This is the fourth edition of this booklet, first published in July 1987. It has been brought up to date in a number of respects. For example, since the last edition the Commission has been given additional responsibilities under the Broadcasting Act. A brief new section has been added on European Community legislation affecting this Commission. Rather more prominence is given to the regulation of privatised industries and the MMC's involvement.

Since its establishment in 1949 the Monopolies and Mergers Commission has played an important part in the industrial and commercial development of this country. During this time its role has expanded considerably.

Its early work was limited to investigating monopolies in the supply of goods. This was later expanded to include services of all kinds and mergers. Further extensions of its work include anti-competitive practices of individual companies, market practices generally, restrictive labour practices, as well as references relating to public sector bodies and newly privatised industries. The common element in all the Commission's work is the assessment of the public interest in relation to healthy competition.

While the Commission is probably well enough known, particularly in the light of a number of publicised reports, I believe that there is a need for a booklet setting out briefly what we do and how we do it. This booklet aims to do just that. For a more detailed description of the legal framework within which we operate, the reader would need to consult the relevant legislation, such as the Fair Trading Act 1973. For the actual detailed work itself the reader should refer to the Commission's reports which can be obtained from HMSO.

I hope that this booklet will provide a useful guide to what we do.

SYDNEY LIPWORTH
Chairman

July 1992

1

The Commission

What is the Monopolies and Mergers Commission?

The Commission is a statutory body set up to inquire into and report on matters which are referred to it. As will be described, these references include, amongst others, questions relating to specific mergers, monopolies, anti-competitive practices, the performance of public sector bodies and the regulation of certain privatised industries.

The Commission is independent of the Government both in its conduct of inquiries and in its conclusions. Its reports are all published. The Commission occupies offices at:
New Court
48 Carey Street
London
WC2A 2JT

When was it established?

The Commission was first set up as the Monopolies and Restrictive Practices Commission in 1949. Its present title and many of the current responsibilities are derived from the Fair Trading Act 1973 (referred to here as the 1973 Act). The Competition Act 1980 (referred to as the 1980 Act), the relevant privatisation statutes and the Broadcasting Act 1990 govern the rest of the Commission's activities.

Of whom does the Commission consist?

The Commission has a full-time Chairman appointed by the Secretary of State for Trade and Industry (referred to throughout as 'the Secretary of State'), whose department is responsible for competition policy. The Secretary of State also appoints the members of the Commission, who are part-time, not more than three of whom are appointed as Deputy Chairmen. At present there are some 34 members, although the ceiling is 50.

Members represent a wealth of experience, including as they do, business men and women, members of the professions, trade union officials and academics. They are paid a salary and are appointed for their individual experience and ability and not as representatives of particular organisations, interests or political persuasions. Members normally serve for an initial three-year term and are eligible for reappointment.

The Commission has a staff of about 100 officials, the senior of whom is the Secretary to the Commission (referred to throughout as 'the Secretary'). About two-thirds are direct employees of the Commission; most of the remainder are on loan from government departments with an increasing use being made of secondments from the business world. The staff include administrators and specialists such as accountants, economists, lawyers and industrial experts, as well as those engaged in support services.

A detailed organisation chart of the Commission and biographical details of members are given in the 1991 Review referred to in the reading list at the end of this booklet.

What type of matters does the Commission inquire into?

Table 1 on page 4 shows the types of inquiries the Commission deals with, the governing legislation for each and by whom the reference is usually made. The Commission has no power to initiate its own investigations.

In the first four decades up to 1989 the Commission produced some 263 reports. Figure 1 shows how these broke down according to type of reference between each of the four decades. Between 1990 and June 1992 the Commission produced a further 57 reports bringing the total up to 320 reports.

Figure 1 Reports published

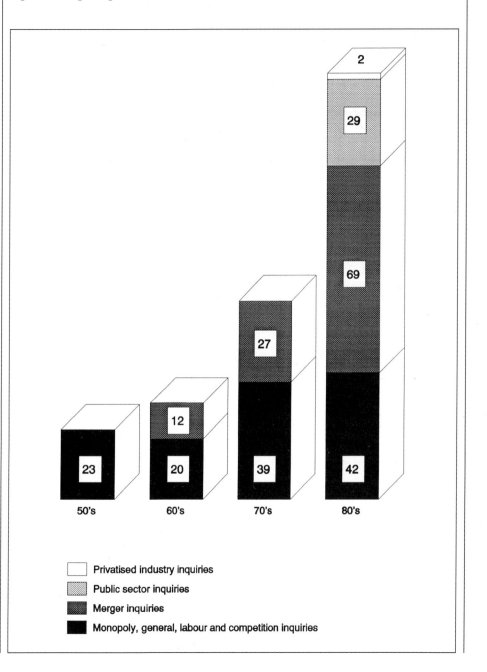

2

29

69

27

12

23   20   39   42

50's   60's   70's   80's

☐ Privatised industry inquiries

▓ Public sector inquiries

▓ Merger inquiries

■ Monopoly, general, labour and competition inquiries

Table 1

Type of inquiry	Governing legislation	Referral usually* made by:
Merger references	Fair Trading Act 1973	Secretary of State for Trade and Industry
Newspaper merger references	,,	,, ,, ,,
Monopoly references	,,	Director General of Fair Trading
General references	,,	Secretary of State for Trade and Industry
Restrictive labour practices references	,,	Ministers
Competition references	Competition Act 1980	Director General of Fair Trading
Public sector references	,,	Secretary of State for Trade and Industry
Privatised industry:		
Telecommunications references	Telecommunications Act 1984	Director General of Telecommunications
Gas references	Gas Act 1986	Director General of Gas Supply
Airports references	Airports Act 1986	Civil Aviation Authority
Water references	Water Act 1989 (now Water Industry Act 1991)	Director General of Water Services
Electricity references	Electricity Act 1989	Director General of Electricity Supply
Broadcasting references	Broadcasting Act 1990	Independent Television Commission or holders of regional Channel 3 licences

* Includes cases where only one person can make the reference, for example, the Secretary of State regarding mergers.

Table 2

	1986	1987	1988	1989	1990	1991
Mergers	6	6	4	13	20*	13
Newspaper mergers	—	1	1	2	1	1
Monopolies	5	2	3	8	4	5
Competition	—	—	—	2	1	—
Public sector	3	3	3	3	2	1
General	—	—	1	—	—	—
Labour	—	—	—	1	—	—
Airports	—	1	—	—	—	1
Telecommunications	—	—	—	1	—	—
	14	13	12	30	28	21

*Three of these were mergers between water undertakings investigated under the Water Act 1989.
Note: Work on some reports published each year will have been partly or wholly done in previous years.

What is the Commission's workload?

Commission inquiries often cover issues of considerable complexity and importance to the national economy. For example, the supply of beer, credit card services and the supply of petrol, all of which were the subject of monopoly inquiries, respectively accounted for about 3.5, 5 and 3.0 per cent of consumer expenditure. The outcome of inquiries is also of crucial importance to the undertakings concerned. All the Commission's investigations must be thorough and based on a full survey of the facts. They are conducted in depth, taking into account a vast amount of written and oral evidence, not only from those directly involved but also from those whose interests may be affected by the outcome. The number of Commission reports published over the last six years is given in Table 2.

How does the Commission set about an inquiry?

Under the 1973 Act the Commission may determine its own procedure for carrying out inquiries,[1] but must take

[1] While examples of procedure in this publication are those generally adopted in the types of inquiries concerned at the date of publication, the Commission's procedures are open to general modification and may anyway be varied in individual inquiries where this seems desirable, in the particular circumstances.

into consideration the representations of all persons appearing to it to have a substantial interest in the subject matter.

There are certain administrative arrangements common to all types of inquiries and these are put in hand as soon as a reference is received. Although all references are made to the Commission as a body, it has been the practice for a group of up to six to be appointed by the Chairman to conduct each inquiry. The minimum number for a group is three.

In choosing members to form each group, care is taken to try and achieve a balance of experience relevant to the subject matter of the inquiry. (There are special arrangements for newspaper mergers and for telecommunications, water and electricity references – see below.) Care is taken to ensure that there is no conflict of interest. The Chairman also appoints one member of the group, generally himself or one of the Deputy Chairmen, to act as chairman of the group.

Meanwhile the Secretary assigns a team of officials to support the group. The team will include such specialist staff as are needed to cover the subject involved. Occasionally, when there is a technical aspect to a reference where additional experience would be helpful, outside advisers are retained for the duration of the inquiry.

What powers does the Commission have to collect evidence?

The Commission has powers to require any person to attend to give evidence or to produce any relevant documents; and to require information from any person carrying on any business (broadly, such as he could be compelled to provide in civil proceedings before a court).

It has very rarely been necessary for the Commission to use these powers, as the persons concerned have fully responded to its requests for information.

It is a criminal offence to furnish any information to the Commission (or to provide such information to another knowing that it is to be used for this purpose) knowing that it is false or misleading in a material particular.

How does one offer evidence to the Commission?

All references are published, and the Commission will normally invite evidence by placing advertisements in the press; people wishing to make their views known on current inquiries are asked to submit them in writing to the Reference Secretary for the inquiry. Some interested parties may then be invited to present their evidence in person.

The Commission does not comment on the substance of current or past inquiries.

How does the Commission treat confidential information?

Under the 1973 Act no information about a business obtained in the course of a Commission inquiry may be disclosed without the consent of the person carrying on that business, subject to certain specific exemptions. The Commission must also have regard to the need to exclude from its reports material relating to the private affairs of an individual or the affairs of a body of persons, where the Commission considers that their interests could be prejudiced by publication.

The important exceptions to these limitations are those arising from the duties laid upon the Commission by law, in particular, its duty to make a report to the Secretary of State with sufficient detail for an understanding of its conclusions. The Act also provides for disclosure of information '...for the purpose of facilitating the performance of any functions of ...the Commission ...'.

When people submitting their views ask for some points to be kept confidential the Commission makes every effort to meet the request. When it is considered necessary to include such evidence in a report, the party concerned is informed accordingly; and told of their right to ask the Secretary of State to excise the point in question from the published report, if the Secretary of State considers that publication may be detrimental to the public interest.

As a general safeguard it may be noted that members and staff of the Commission – and any outside specialists temporarily retained – are all bound by the Official Secrets Act and by specific provisions of the 1973 and other relevant Acts.

How does the Commission make its reports?

All reports under the 1973 and 1980 Acts are submitted to the Secretary of State. They are signed by all the members of the group concerned and by the Secretary. There is sometimes a division of opinion within the group so occasionally a report contains a Note of Dissent signed by one or more members. In the event of a tied vote the group chairman has a second vote. A two-thirds majority in support of an adverse finding is necessary if this is to be the subject of the Secretary of State's order-making powers.

The Commission sends a copy of its report in the case of monopoly, merger (other than newspaper merger) and competition references to the Director General of Fair Trading (referred to throughout as 'the Director General').

Are the Commission's reports made public?

All reports by the Commission under the 1973 and 1980 Acts must be laid before Parliament and published. They are published intact except for any excisions authorised by the Secretary of State on public interest grounds. Such excisions are indicated in the published report by asterisks or brackets. Reports made under these Acts are sold by Her Majesty's Stationery Office. Provisions for publication exist under the privatisation Acts.

Questions relating either to reports submitted to the Secretary of State and awaiting publication, or to reports already published, should be addressed to the Department of Trade and Industry. The Press Office at the Monopolies and Mergers Commission is available to answer questions about the Commission itself, its procedures, inquiries in progress, etc (see Contact Points, page 28).

2

Merger references

What is a merger?

Of all the types of reference to the Commission, mergers usually attract the most attention in the press. Much of the procedure for handling them relates also to other types of reference and is therefore described in some detail below.

A merger giving rise to a reference to the Commission often involves the acquisition, or prospective acquisition, of control of one company (and the enterprise or enterprises which it carries on) by another. It is most dramatically illustrated by a takeover bid by one company for another.

The expression 'control' may refer to a *controlling interest* which can usually, in practice, be treated as over 50 per cent of the relevant voting power. However, 'control' may also include, in the absence of a controlling interest, the ability *materially to influence the policy* or the ability to *control the policy* of a company or of any person carrying on an enterprise.

Merger references may be made following the completion of a merger but, are more often made in anticipation of one. This typically occurs where there has been an offer by one company to the shareholders of another, with a view to acquiring control of the latter.

For a merger situation to qualify for investigation by the MMC, the criteria are that two or more enterprises (at least one of which is carried on, 'in the United Kingdom or by or under the control of a body corporate incorporated in the United Kingdom') cease to be distinct and that either one or both of the market share test and the assets test are satisfied. An 'enterprise' means the activities, or part of the activities, of a business.

The market share and assets tests are, respectively:

- that as a result of the merger, at least 25 per cent of goods or services of any description which are supplied in the United Kingdom, or in a substantial part of it, are supplied by or to (in the case of services, by or for) a person or, if this was already the case, such supply is enhanced; or
- that the gross value of world-wide assets taken over exceeds £30 million.

Where the necessary conditions are satisfied there is (either actually or prospectively) a merger situation qualifying for investigation. A merger cannot normally be referred to the Commission more than six months after it has occurred.

All merger offers for quoted companies are subject to the City Code on Take-overs and Mergers. This is not a statutory code. It is primarily concerned with the handling of the transaction and the fair treatment of shareholders. Under the Code, the offer must lapse if the merger is referred to the Commission before it becomes unconditional as to acceptances. The bidder may then announce whether it remains his intention to acquire the target company if the merger is cleared by the Commission.

Why are some mergers referred and not others?

The assumption underlying the 1973 Act is that some mergers may have economic, social or other effects which go beyond the interests of the shareholders concerned and merit examination on public interest grounds.

If the market share test or the assets test appears to be satisfied, the Office of Fair Trading (OFT) endeavours to establish the likely effect of the merger, primarily upon competition, but also upon any other matter that might be of concern to the public interest. The OFT's function here is to assist the Director General in making his decision whether or not to advise the Secretary of State that there are sufficient public interest reasons for an in-depth investigation of a particular case by the Commission.[1]

It is important to note that there is no presumption in the Act that a merger is undesirable. The Commission is required to report on whether (if it finds that a merger situation has been or would be created) the merger situation operates, or may be expected to operate, against the public interest. In making its finding the Commission will take into account any benefits which may appear to arise from the merger.

---

[1] For a detailed account see the OFT's booklet, *Mergers: a guide to the procedures under the Fair Trading Act 1973.* ·

What is meant by 'the public interest'?

Section 84 of the 1973 Act requires that the Commission when considering the public interest, 'shall take into account all matters which appear to them in the particular circumstances to be relevant'; and, among other things, have regard to five points which, summarised, are:

- maintaining and promoting competition in the United Kingdom;
- promoting the interests of consumers;
- promoting through competition the development of new products and the reduction of costs;
- maintaining and promoting the balanced distribution of industry and employment; and
- maintaining and promoting competitive activity in overseas markets by companies in the United Kingdom.

What proportion of mergers is referred?

A relatively small number of mergers scrutinised by the OFT are referred to the Commission as is shown in Table 3. Many of these will, however, be among the larger mergers which often raise the most wide-ranging competition issues – though this is now subject to the effect of the European Community Merger Regulation (see page 27) in causing some substantial mergers to be investigated instead by the European Commission. It should also be remembered that the cases which the OFT examines are themselves only a proportion – about one-third – of all mergers.

Table 3

Merger proposals	1986	1987	1988	1989	1990	1991
Number of qualifying mergers	313	321	306	281	261	183
Referred to Commission	13	6	11	14	25	7
Abandoned before Commission report	7	0	2	2	3	1

What happens if it is decided that a merger merits investigation?

The Director General has the responsibility under the Act to recommend to the Secretary of State whether a merger should be referred to the Commission. The Secretary of State makes his decision in the light of that advice. The decision is announced and in appropriate cases reasons may be given. The Secretary of State may explain what particular aspect of a merger seems to him to warrant an inquiry. The Commission is not constrained by the mention of any such grounds, and the question as to whether a merger is detrimental to the public interest is for the Commission, as an independent body, to investigate.

What form does a merger reference take?

The reference states that it appears to the Secretary of State that a merger situation has been created in that enterprises carried on by or under the control of named companies have ceased to be distinct, or that arrangements are in progress, or in contemplation, which have or would have that result.

The reference specifies that either the assets test or the market share test appears to be satisfied (it is more often the assets test, which is easier to establish at this early stage), and asks the Commission to investigate and report on whether a merger situation has been (or, if arrangements are carried into effect, would be) created and, if so, whether this would operate or might be expected to operate against the public interest.

If, after a reference has been made, the bidder abandons his proposal, the Commission can ask for the reference to be laid aside. Occasionally, an unwilling target company may seek out another company with which it would prefer to merge – a 'White Knight'; or another bidder, welcome or not, may appear. There have been occasions when another offer has been made in the course of an inquiry. If that situation is also referred there would then be two simultaneous inquiries. If the new merger does not qualify for reference, or if it is not referred, and if it succeeds – then the first bidder might seek to have the original reference laid aside. More usually, an inquiry runs its course.

How does the Commission inquire into a merger?

The first thing to establish is that there is a merger situation in existence, in progress, or in contemplation and that the merger situation qualifies for investigation. The main parties to the merger, that is, the bidding company and the target company, are asked to make written submissions of their case for the merger – or against it, when it is contested. (They will be told what information given to the OFT the Commission has seen and that this need not be repeated.) The Commission's staff will follow up with requests for any further information needed by the group of members appointed to the reference. Often the group visits the companies concerned, for a better understanding of the background.

The Commission invites submissions from other parties it thinks may have views on the merger, such as suppliers, customers or competitors, and the trades unions concerned.

At regular meetings the group of members, with the advice and assistance of its supporting staff, discuss the evidence and views obtained and formulate possible public interest issues. As explained above, the Commission shall take all relevant matters into account, but the key issue has in most cases been competition[1].

The main parties are informed of the issues together with any evidence of other persons to which a response from the parties is sought by the group.

As soon as practicable the two companies, and some of the third parties, are invited to meetings with the group – known as hearings. The main purpose of the hearing is to examine the key issues raised by the merger. All hearings are held in private, generally with each party appearing separately. They are relatively informal. They are conducted as an investigation, and not in an adversarial manner. The group is

[1]A publication, *Assessing Competition,* is available free from the Commission (see reading list). This briefly describes some of the issues the Commission considers when assessing competition in its inquiries.

acting as fact-finder and judge of the issues, not as prosecutor. Although it is not required, parties may be legally represented if they so wish. A transcript is taken of each hearing and a copy is sent to the party concerned for checking for accuracy.

It may then be necessary to hold subsequent meetings with each main party in order to discuss further certain issues and, where appropriate to the developing conclusions, possible safeguards for the public interest. The main parties are given every opportunity to explain their cases.

How long does a merger inquiry take?

An initial period of up to six months is allowed for in the Act and the exact time is specified in the reference. In recent years the period of inquiries has been reduced to around three months. The Commission can request from the Secretary of State one extension of up to three months, if there are special reasons why the report cannot be made within the specified period.

The Commission makes every effort to complete the inquiry and report as quickly as possible, consistently with thoroughness and fairness. Time must be allowed for all parties to prepare and present their cases and for the Commission to weigh all the evidence. The Commission has a duty to act fairly and, while in the nature of things not all its conclusions are received with universal approval, the Commission is at pains to show that it has reached them with care and impartiality.

How does the Commission report its findings on a merger?

A merger report will open with a summary of the report. It will then include a brief description of each of the main companies, the background to the merger and the market in which the companies operate, the views of interested parties and of the main parties concerned and, finally, a conclusions chapter. Drafts of factual material and views expressed will normally have been put back to the originators, who are asked to confirm their accuracy.

All but the summary and the final chapter is essentially background, but as it constitutes material upon which the group has based its conclusions it is desirable to make it publicly available. It is also required in order to explain those conclusions to the Secretary of State. (While initially most readers probably turn to the summary or the conclusions, in the longer term the background material is widely referred to for information on companies and markets.)

The conclusions chapter normally confirms that the statutory criteria for a merger qualifying for investigation are satisfied. It explains what public interest issues arise and in what way; and whether or not any aspect of the merger operates or may be expected to operate against the public interest.

If the Commission does make any adverse findings it may make any recommendations it sees fit to remedy or prevent those adverse effects it considers arise from the merger. The Commission may recommend that the merger should not be allowed to take place, or, if it has already taken place, that there should be divestment.

Alternatively, the Commission may recommend that the merger should not be allowed unless the bidder gives some enforceable undertakings. Undertakings may include divestment of all or part of the shareholding, or of certain assets or businesses of the target company, or relate to future behaviour.

What action is taken on the Commission's report?

The Commission's report is made to the Secretary of State. If it has found that the merger does not operate, or may be expected not to operate, against the public interest, the Secretary of State has no power under the Act to overrule the conclusion. Where the merger has not already taken place the bidder is free, so far as the requirements of the 1973 Act are concerned, to make a new offer, which it will be up to the target company's shareholders to accept or reject.

If the Commission has found against the merger, the Secretary of State must take into account any recommendations made in the report (for example, that the merger should not be allowed to go ahead). He also takes account of any advice that the Director General offers. The Secretary of State is not bound to accept the Commission's recommendation, but has usually done so.

An announcement of the Secretary of State's decision is generally made at the time the report is published and laid before Parliament. He may ask the Director General to seek undertakings from the parties; for example, not to proceed with the merger or, where the merger has taken place, from the acquirer, to dispose of all or part of any existing shareholding in, or assets of, the target company. Alternatively, he may require particular undertakings to be given as a condition of the merger going ahead. The Secretary of State also has powers under the 1973 Act to impose remedies by order.

The Director General is responsible for seeking any undertakings required; and for keeping under review any undertakings given or orders made in respect of mergers, and for advising the Secretary of State if further action seems necessary.

What is different about newspaper mergers?

Special provisions apply to newspaper mergers. The Secretary of State's consent is required to a transfer of newspapers or newspaper assets which concentrates, in the hands of one newspaper proprietor, newspapers with an average paid-for circulation of 500,000 or more copies per day of circulation. A newspaper proprietor can be, for example, any person controlling one-quarter of the voting power of a body corporate which is an actual newspaper proprietor. That consent cannot be given (except in certain urgent or *de minimis* cases) before the Commission has investigated and reported.

In such an investigation the Commission proceeds along much the same lines as for other merger references. It is recognised, however, that newspaper mergers are important for more than economic reasons; section 59(3) of the 1973 Act requires the Commission to take into account all matters which appear in the circumstances to be relevant and particularly the need for accurate presentation of news and free expression of opinion.

The Secretary of State maintains a panel of persons with particular experience, from whom he may appoint one, two or three members to join the group of Commission members solely for the purpose of considering a newspaper merger.

The Director General is not involved.

The time taken by the Commission for investigating newspaper merger references may be from two to three months with one possible extension of up to three months if there are special reasons.

3

Monopoly references

What is a monopoly?

In this context a monopoly is *not* what a dictionary may say it is, that is 'exclusive possession of the trade in some commodity'.

The 1973 Act provides for two separate kinds of monopoly situations:

- *scale* – where at least 25 per cent of goods or services of any description supplied in the United Kingdom (or in a defined part of it) is supplied by or to (in the case of services, by or for) a person, company or members of an interconnected group of companies; and

- *complex* – where at least 25 per cent of goods or services of any description supplied in the United Kingdom (or in a defined part of it) is supplied by or to (in the case of services, by or for) persons or companies who are members of a group (not being an interconnected group of companies) who, whether voluntarily or not, by agreement or otherwise, conduct their respective affairs in such a way as to prevent, restrict or distort competition in connection with the production or supply of such goods or the supply of such services; the goods or services concerned need not necessarily be supplied by or to (or for) every member of such a group.[1]

---

[1]Agreements which are registrable under the Restrictive Trade Practices Act 1976 are (to that extent), outside the Commission's jurisdiction in monopoly and some other inquiries, for example, under the 1980 Act.

There is no presumption in the legislation that it is wrong to be a monopolist. For example, if a person invents and patents a new gadget and sets up a firm to make it, he is necessarily a total monopolist – but he may well have performed a public service. The 1973 Act merely recognises that when a monopoly situation exists, there is the possibility of prejudice to the public interest. That possibility can only be confirmed by investigation.

How is a monopoly reference made?

Monopoly references are usually made by the Director General rather than by the Secretary of State, and often as the result of allegations of anti-competitive behaviour received by the OFT. It is not necessary for it to be established prior to the reference that the monopoly in question exists (although in practice the Director General has *prima facie* grounds for believing that, as defined, it does). While the party or parties which may appear to occupy a monopoly position are not named in the terms of reference, it may sometimes state what practices the Commission is to investigate.

This broad-brush approach leaves it to the Commission to investigate the market as a whole. This will often be a major exercise, and the Commission was in the past given as much as 24 months in which to report. In recent years the procedure has been accelerated. It is more usual now for the period to be about twelve months or nine months, and it may be less. The co-operation of all concerned is essential in order to meet the resulting deadlines.

The reference specifies the goods or service to which it relates, and asks the Commission to establish whether a monopoly situation exists; and, if so, in favour of what person or persons (the monopolist). It usually goes on to ask whether there are any steps, by way of uncompetitive practices or otherwise, being taken by the monopolist to exploit or maintain the monopoly situation; and whether any action or omission on their part is attributable to that situation, and if so, how. According to the 1973 Act, 'uncompetitive practices' means those practices which have the effect of preventing, restricting or distorting competition in connection with any commercial activities in the United Kingdom. Sometimes the Commission is asked to investigate only a specific practice, such as 'prices charged' or 'any refusal to supply'.

A monopoly reference also usually asks whether any facts found by the Commission in its inquiry operate, or may be expected to operate, against the public interest.

How does the Commission handle a monopoly reference?

In many ways as it handles a merger reference. A group is appointed, facts collected and views invited. It is usually the case that one company, or a small number of companies, appear to occupy an important or dominant position in the market being investigated and it is likely that some of the evidence from other parties will include complaints about alleged practices by such companies.

The Commission will frequently seek information about the market and the alleged practices by means of questionnaires. Apart from details of the activities of the companies concerned, including their pricing policies, profitability etc, the Commission may need to ask about ownership of subsidiaries, or of interests in competitors, formal or informal links or agreements with companies here or abroad and membership of trade bodies.

Smaller questionnaires may be sent to companies or bodies occupying less prominent positions in the market concerned, and to other interested parties; any of whom may in due course be asked to attend separate hearings with the Commission.

There is a balance to be struck initially between casting the questionnaire net too wide and, on the other hand, at a later stage finding more questions to be necessary, causing inconvenience to the parties and delaying the conclusion of the inquiry.

After assembling the facts, the Commission will write to the relevant companies informing them that they have been provisionally identified as monopolists. Additionally, (at the same time or later), main parties will be given: (i) the public interest issues which, at that time, the Commission believes may arise from the monopoly situation which has been provisionally found to exist and which require consideration; (ii) a summary of the facts about the market; and (iii) a summary of any criticisms that have been put to the Commission by third parties.

The parties are usually requested to reply with their comments in writing within a month (or such other period as may seem appropriate in the circumstances to the Commission), after which they are usually invited, separately, to attend hearings at the Commission with the group. The principal aim of these hearings is to discuss the potential public interest issues outlined in the letter. Although it is not required, companies may be legally represented if they wish. Additional meetings are held as necessary, for example, for further discussion of the possible issues, or to put to main parties criticisms from elsewhere, or to deal with any other matters which seem to the group to be appropriate including possible safeguards for the public interest.

How is a report made on a monopoly reference?

The report is made to the Secretary of State. It is similar to a merger report in that it will include a summary, a description of the market and of the company (or companies) concerned and the views of the monopolist(s) and other parties.

The report must give definite conclusions on the questions asked in the reference, namely whether there is a monopoly situation and in whose favour, and on any other questions, for example, whether there are any steps, by way of uncompetitive practices or otherwise, being taken by the monopolist to exploit or maintain the monopoly situation. If the report states that any facts found operate, or may be expected to operate, against the public interest, and identifies particular effects adverse to that interest, it may include recommendations for action, either by public authorities (for example, Ministers) or by the monopolist(s), which could remedy or prevent those effects. Recommendations may, for example, relate to the ending of certain agreements, publication of prices or other information, division of businesses, disposal of shareholdings and the prohibiting of any tie-in of the supply of certain goods and services.

What action is taken following a monopoly report?

The Secretary of State lays the report before Parliament and usually announces what steps if any he is taking. Where the Commission has concluded that there are particular effects adverse to the public interest, the Secretary of State, having considered any recommendations made by the Commission and any advice given by the Director General, may make an order to remedy or prevent those effects. More often he may pursue the alternative route of asking the Director General to negotiate satisfactory undertakings with the parties concerned.

It is the function of the Director General to keep the operation of any orders made or undertakings given under review and to advise the Secretary of State should he conclude that they require modification in the light of changed circumstances.

At the same time that the report is laid before Parliament it is published.

4

Competition references

What is the difference between a monopoly reference and a competition reference?

A monopoly reference requires the Commission to investigate a whole market and – if they are there to be found – in substance identify any uncompetitive practices and their effects on the public interest. The Competition Act 1980 introduced a new process which could focus on a specific practice. As was said in Parliament during the passage of the Bill that became the 1980 Act:

For the first time an individual practice by an individual firm can be thoroughly investigated and if it is an anti-competitive practice it can be stopped should that practice be against the public interest.

To establish whether there is a course of conduct which constitutes what the 1980 Act termed an anti-competitive practice, that is, it has or is intended to have or likely to have the effect of restricting, distorting or preventing competition,

the Director General conducts his own examination and publishes a report of his findings. If these establish that the conduct amounts to an anti-competitive practice he may accept undertakings from any person the report has named, if he finds those undertakings to be a sufficient remedy. He must then publish the undertakings and keep their observance under review.[1]

Failing satisfactory undertakings – or their observance – the Director General may make a reference to the Commission naming the person or persons concerned, the goods or services involved and the course of conduct to be investigated. The Commission may be given up to six months within which to report, though one extension of not more than three months can be granted by the Secretary of State.

What sort of anti-competitive practices are referred?

Not many competition references have been made, partly due to the number of undertakings satisfactorily concluded between the OFT and the companies concerned. Examples of references made include, in 1982, the London Electricity Board and its sale of domestic electrical goods through its retail showrooms in such a way as to give rise to persistent losses; and, in 1984, the policy of the Ford Motor Company of not granting licences to manufacture or sell in the United Kingdom certain

---

[1] See the OFT's free booklet *Anti-competitive practices: a guide to the provisions of the Competition Act 1980.*

replacement body parts for Ford vehicles. In 1989 the Commission examined Black & Decker's supply policies in response to alleged loss leading by its retailers, and also Unichem's share allotment scheme, while in 1990, it inquired into the over-provision of bus services in the Inverness area by Highland Scottish Omnibuses.

How does the Commission handle a competition reference?

Again, the procedure is similar to that of a merger reference referred to above.

In making its report to the Secretary of State, the Commission must state whether any person named in the reference was, at any time in the 12 months immediately preceding the reference, pursuing in relation to the goods or services specified in the reference the course of conduct so specified, or one which was similar. It must confirm whether this conduct constituted an anti-competitive practice, and, if so, whether the practice operated or might be expected to operate against the public interest.

If the Commission so finds it must specify what are, or are likely to be, the effects adverse to the public interest; consider what action might be taken to remedy them, and recommend any steps that should be taken by the party concerned and, where appropriate, by Ministers. These might, for example, include ending discriminatory practices.

What action follows a report on a competition reference?

Upon receipt of the Commission's report concluding that any person specified was engaging in an anti-competitive practice which operated or might be expected to operate against the public interest, the Secretary of State will take account of any advice given him by the Director General. If it appears to the Secretary of State that any adverse effects could be remedied by certain action being taken or abstained from, he has power under the 1980 Act to require compliance by order. Alternatively, he may ask the Director General to secure undertakings to that end from the person concerned.

If the Director General secures no satisfactory undertakings, or if they are not fulfilled, the Secretary of State may use his order making powers accordingly.

5

Public sector references

What is the purpose of public sector references?

Section 11 of the 1980 Act empowers the Secretary of State to refer to the Commission any question relating to the efficiency and costs of, the service provided by, or the possible abuse of a monopoly situation by nationalised industries and certain other public sector bodies such as the Post Office, British Rail and London Underground.

With very few exceptions such bodies are not accountable as is a public limited company to shareholders. In the public sector there is often little effective competition, and even where a public body has no monopoly it is not subject to the full rigours of the market place and the commercial incentives to efficiency which that can provide.

Parliament therefore considered it important that what are in effect efficiency audits of such bodies should be carried out periodically. Such references have represented a major and important part of the Commission's work, although because of privatisation the number of undertakings subject to review has declined.

The terms of reference for each inquiry may also require the Commission to report on whether the body concerned is pursuing a course of conduct which operates against the public interest; this is conventionally included since an adverse public interest finding is the trigger to the use, if appropriate, of statutory follow-up powers contained in section 12 of the Act.

How is a public sector reference made and investigated?

The reference is made by the Secretary of State, after consultation with the appropriate Minister if responsibility for the industry concerned lies with another department. The Commission may be given up to six months in which to make its report. One extension of up to three months can be granted by the Secretary of State.

Detailed requests for information are made to the organisation. Commission staff carry out fieldwork and members and staff visit the organisation's offices and establishments. Meetings will be held with trade unions and other interested bodies – often including those representing the interests of users of the organisation's services or products.

Commission staff then identify what appear to be the main issues and the facts underlying them. These serve as background for the group to hold its first full discussions with the organisation, which is informed in advance of the general topics to be covered. The purpose is to test the findings, to discuss the views of the management on current trends and future developments and to have their response to any criticisms.

Further meetings of the group will then develop tentative conclusions and recommendations. These are normally conveyed to the organisation so that, if it wishes, it may submit a written response before attending a further meeting at which these tentative conclusions and recommendations will be discussed.

The trade unions may be invited back again to discuss matters which might become conclusions in areas of direct concern to them, for example, industrial relations, manning levels etc.

What form does a public sector report take?

Apart from specifying the scope of the Commission's inquiry the typical terms of reference include a number of questions drawing its attention to particular matters the Commission should investigate. Section 11(8) of the 1980 Act requires the Commission to exclude from its investigation and report consideration of any question relating to the appropriateness of the financial obligations, or guidance as to financial objectives, imposed on or given to the undertaking under any enactment or otherwise by a Minister and certain questions within the scope of the Restrictive Trade Practices Act 1976.

The main areas of inquiry will include investment policies and procedures, the control and use of manpower and other resources, management information systems, fares or pricing policies, matching supply and demand, maintenance performance and quality of service.

The opening assessment chapter of the Commission's report on a public sector inquiry summarises the whole report. It provides an overview and summarises the main conclusions with, where appropriate, the corresponding recommendations – with an indication of the main priorities. It also answers the basic questions in the terms of reference about the undertaking's efficiency and costs and the service provided.

The bulk of the rest of the report consists of factual chapters relating to the main areas of inquiry, each ending with a number of conclusions reached by the group with, where appropriate, a corresponding recommendation. Such recommendations may, for example, cover the provision of services, costs, management structure and performance indicators and targets. Where appropriate, deadlines for implementation will be set as well as an indication of priority.

The Commission is concerned that its recommendations should be feasible; their implementation capable of being checked; and that they should relate to best practice rather than to an abstract ideal. From the expertise available within the Commission, and with experience of successive inquiries, a wide ranging data base of best practice in both the public and private sectors has been built up, and is still being extended.

The Commission's report is delivered to the Secretary of State, who is formally responsible for its printing, publication and laying before Parliament.

What action follows a public sector reference?

Following publication of the report the industry concerned is normally required to give its initial response to the Commission's recommendations within three to four months. This is followed by a further statement after 12 months explaining the action taken and the results achieved. These responses are announced to Parliament and copies are placed in the library of the House of Commons. Once follow-up action has been completed the industry will produce a final response no later than three years after the Commission's original report, recording in full what has been done.

6

General references

The Secretary of State, together with other Ministers if appropriate, may, under section 78 of the 1973 Act, require the Commission to report on the general effect on the public interest of any practice which appears to him to be uncompetitive, or of practices which, in his opinion, are commonly adopted as a result of, or to preserve, a monopoly situation. He may also ask for a report on the desirability of any specified action to deal with such practices or actions, or on the effects or potential effects of monopoly situations. No powers flow from a report on a general reference.

The most recent of the seven such references so far received was in March 1988. The report on this reference, *Collective licensing: a report on certain practices in the collective licensing of public performance and broadcasting rights in sound recordings,* was published in December 1988.

7

Restrictive labour practices references

Under section 79 of the 1973 Act the Secretary of State, together with other Ministers if appropriate, may refer to the Commission questions whether a specified practice exists and, if so, whether it is a restrictive labour practice; and, if it is, whether it operates or may be expected to operate against the public interest; and, finally with what, if any, adverse effects.

A restrictive labour practice in this context refers (to simplify) to any restrictions not exclusively relating to remuneration, connected with employment or work done in specified commercial activities in the United Kingdom, which are not necessary or are more stringent than necessary, and which could be discontinued without contravening any legal requirement.

The first, and so far only, reference to the Commission under this section was made in March 1988. The report on this reference, *Labour practices in TV and Film making,* was published in April 1989.

Again, no powers flow from such a report.

8

Privatised sector inquiries

Since 1984 a new duty has been laid upon the Commission, that of conducting inquiries under statutes giving effect to the privatisation of undertakings formerly in the public sector. Currently these new duties relate to telecommunications, gas, certain airports, water and electricity.

All these undertakings require formal authority, usually given by the appropriate Minister or regulator, setting out the conditions upon which the activity concerned may be carried out. This authority is variously referred to as a licence (telecommunications and electricity), authorisation (gas), permission (airports) and appointment (water).

Apart from specific instances relating to airports and water (described below), references to the Commission by the regulators arise when a decision by the regulator to modify a condition (or conditions) of a licence, authorisation etc. governing the operation of that industry is disputed by the licence holder. No references arise where such modification is agreed between the regulator and the holder of a licence.

The time taken by the Commission for investigating privatised industry references is six months with the possibility of one extension of up to six months.

9

Telecommunications references

Under the Telecommunications Act 1984, the Director General of Telecommunications may make a telecommunication licence modification reference to the Commission. Such a reference requires the Commission to investigate and report on matters relating to the provision of telecommunication services or the supply of telecommunication apparatus by a person authorised by a licence under section 7 of the Act to operate a telecommunication system. Such matters may also include the price control regime, reviewed by the Director General of Telecommunications in 1988 after the first five years of operation, and subsequently reviewed every four years.

The Commission's report is made to the Director General of Telecommunications. If the Commission finds that the matters in question do not operate against the public interest that decision is final. However, where the Commission concludes that any such matters operate, or may be expected to operate, against the public interest and that any adverse effects could be remedied or prevented by the conditions of the licence being modified,

the Director General of Telecommunications is required, having regard to modifications which are specified in the report, to make such modifications as appear requisite to him for remedying or preventing the adverse effects.

As with the other privatised undertakings the public interest test is specifically provided for in the Act which says the Commission shall have regard to the matters as respects which duties are imposed on the Secretary of State and the Director General of Telecommunications. These include, for example, promotion of the interests of consumers, purchasers and other users in respect of prices and services; the maintenance and promotion of effective competition; the promotion of efficiency and economy; and the promotion of research and development.

The Secretary of State maintains a panel of at least three persons with particular experience – the Telecommunications Panel – from whom the Chairman of the Commission is required to appoint at least one member to join the group investigating such a reference.

The first reference under this Act, relating to chatlines and message services, was made on 19 July 1988. The report, *Chatlines and Message Services,* was published in February 1989.

10

Gas references

Under the Gas Act 1986, the Director General of Gas Supply may, as one of his functions, refer to the Commission questions relating to the supply of gas by a public gas supplier to tariff customers. (The Competition and Service (Utilities) Act 1992 extended this function to the transmission, distribution and storage of gas.) Such questions may include proposed modifications to the price control formula which is reviewed every five years by the Director General of Gas Supply.

The regulatory regime for gas distinguishes between the tariff and contract sectors of the gas supply market. In broad terms, tariff customers are those who take not more than 25,000 therms a year and, for the most part, are in the domestic sector, while most industrial and commercial customers, who take more than 25,000 therms a year, fall into the contract sector.

The Commission's report is made to the Director General of Gas Supply. If the Commission finds that the matters in question do not operate against the public interest that decision is final. However, if the Commission concludes that any of the matters specified in the reference operate or may be expected to operate against the public interest and that any adverse effects could be remedied or prevented by the conditions of the authorisation being modified, the Director General of Gas Supply is required to make such modifications as appear requisite to him for remedying or preventing the adverse effects. He must have regard to modifications which are specified in the report.

Although the Director General of Gas Supply does not have the power to refer to the Commission matters relating to gas supply to contract customers, this sector can be made the subject of references under the 1973 Act. Thus in November 1987, the supply of gas to non-tariff customers was the subject of a monopoly reference made to the Commission by the Director General of Fair Trading. The report, *Gas,* was published in October 1988.

11

Airport references

Under the Airports Act 1986 certain aspects of the economic regulation of airports may be referred to the Commission by the Civil Aviation Authority (the CAA).

This Act provided, among other things, for the privatisation of the British Airports Authority (now BAA plc) and for the constitution of the larger local authority airports as companies. Broadly, all airports with an annual turnover exceeding £1 million were (to simplify) made subject to economic regulation by the CAA. Designated airports were also made subject to mandatory references to the Commission every five years. To date the three BAA plc London airports (Heathrow, Gatwick and Stansted) and Manchester airport, operated by Manchester Airport plc, have been so designated.

The five-yearly references for designated airports require the Commission to investigate and report to the CAA on the maximum amounts which are capable of being levied by the airport operator by way of airport charges. These charges are levied on operators of aircraft in connection with the landing, parking or taking off of aircraft at the airport including passenger charges. The references also require the Commission to investigate and report on whether the operator has pursued courses of conduct which have operated or might be expected to operate against the public interest. The Commission's report is made to the CAA which must accept the public interest finding and otherwise have regard to recommendations made in the report.

The CAA may also make references to the Commission if, following its own investigation of a complaint, it is unable to agree an appropriate remedy with the airport concerned.

The first reference to the Commission under this Act was a quinquennial type reference made in respect of Manchester Airport plc in 1987; the second quinquennial reference was made in December 1991. The reports were published by the CAA in December 1987 and July 1992 respectively. In December 1990, the CAA asked the Commission to inquire into the economic regulation of the South-East airports companies. The Commission's report, *BAA plc,* was published by the CAA in July 1991.

12

Water references

Under the Water Industry Act 1991, which amended the 1989 Water Act, the Director General of Water Services (DGWS) may refer to the Commission questions about matters relating to the carrying out of a water company's functions under its appointment, (a term which corresponds to a telecommunication licence or public gas supplier's authorisation). The Commission's report is made to the (DGWS).

If the Commission finds that the matters in question do not operate against the public interest that decision is final. However, if the Commission concludes that any of the matters specified in the reference operate or may be expected to operate against the public interest and that any adverse effects could be remedied or prevented by the

conditions of the appointment being modified, the DGWS is required, having regard to modifications which are specified in the report, to make such modifications as appear requisite to him for remedying or preventing the adverse effects.

As with the other privatised undertakings the public interest test is specifically provided for in the Act, which says the Commmission shall have regard to the matters as respects which duties are imposed on the Secretary of State and the DGWS by the Act. These include the charges made for services provided and other costs levied by water or sewerage undertakers, with particular concern to ensure that there is no discrimination in respect of the interests of customers in rural areas; quality of services provided, protection of land rights; promotion of economy and efficiency; and promotion of effective competition.

Under the terms of appointment of the water companies, the DGWS is obliged to review charges for water supply and sewerage services applied to each water company, having regard to comparative competition, at least every ten years, and every five years if either he or a water company wishes. If the company disputes his determination, the DGWS is required to make a reference to the Commission. The Commission will then determine the matter referred and, if necessary, the condition will be modified accordingly. Unlike other privatised industry references, the outcome of such a reference under the charging provisions in the water companies' appointments is decisive.

The Secretary of State maintains a panel of at least eight persons with particular experience – the Water Panel – from whom the Chairman of the Commission may appoint up to three members to join the group investigating such references.

Finally, under the 1991 Act, the Secretary of State must refer to the Commission certain mergers or proposed mergers involving two or more 'water enterprises' when the value of the assets taken over exceeds £30 million. Under the Act, as amended by the Competition and Service (Utilities) Act 1992, the Commission in considering whether any such merger operates or may be expected to operate against the public interest must have special regard to the principle that the DGWS's ability to make comparisons between different such enterprises should not be prejudiced.

13

Electricity references

The Electricity Act 1989 provides for the industry's regulator, the Director General of Electricity Supply, to be able to refer to the Commission questions on any matters relating to the generation, transmission or supply of electricity in pursuance of a licence to carry out these activities. Such questions may include proposed modifications to the price control formula which will be initially reviewed after five years (or three years for the National Grid Company) by the Director General of Electricity Supply.

The Commission's report is made to the Director General of Electricity Supply. If the Commission finds that the matters in question do not operate against the public interest that decision is final. However, if the Commission concludes that any of the matters specified in the reference operate or may be expected to operate against the public interest and that any adverse effects could be remedied or prevented by the conditions of the licence being modified, the Director General of Electricity Supply is required to make such modifications as appear requisite to him for remedying or preventing the adverse effects. He must have regard to modifications which are specified in the report.

As with the other privatised undertakings the public interest test is specifically provided for in the Act. This says the Commission shall have regard to the matters as respects which duties are imposed on the Secretary of State and the Director General of Electricity Supply. These include, for example, the promotion of competition in the generation and supply of electricity; the protection of the interests of consumers in respect of prices and services; the promotion of efficiency and economy; the promotion of research and development; and the protection of the public from dangers arising from the generation, transmission and supply of electricity.

The Secretary of State maintains a panel of at least eight persons with particular experience – the Electricity Panel – from whom the Chairman of the Commission may appoint up to three members to join the group investigating such a reference.

14

Broadcasting references

Under the Broadcasting Act 1990, the Commission has a new role relating to the competition aspects of networking arrangements between holders of regional Channel 3 licences. Following an investigation by the Director General of Fair Trading, the Independent Television Commission or a licence holder may refer to the Commission, for investigation and report certain questions relating particularly to the competition test described in the Act. The Commission's decision is determinative.

15

European Community Competition Law

The principal competition provisions of the Treaty of Rome are Articles 85 and 86. Article 85(1) prohibits all agreements which have as their object or effect the prevention, restriction or distortion of competition within the European Community (EC). Exemptions can be granted by the European Commission under Article 85(3). Article 86 prohibits any undertaking with a dominant position from abusing that position; under both Articles there has also to be an effect on trade between member states. The procedures of the European Commission in exercising its general powers to enforce Articles 85 and 86 are laid down by Regulation 17 of 1962.

Although the MMC does not normally deal with the assessment of restrictive agreements, various regulations have been enacted by the EC giving group (or block) exemptions under Article 85(3) to certain types of agreements, such as selective distribution agreements for motor cars and exclusive purchasing agreements for beer and petrol, which have to be taken into account in the course of monopoly references. In framing their recommendations in references involving such agreements the MMC must therefore take account of such EC exemptions and their relevance to any suggested changes to practices within the United Kingdom.

Articles 85 and 86 make no specific provision for control by the European Commission of concentrations or mergers 'with a Community dimension'. The EC therefore adopted a European Merger Regulation (Regulation 4064/89), which came into force on 21 September 1990, whereby mergers in this category are subject to the exclusive jurisdiction of the European Commission (save for limited exceptions). Broadly this means that mergers involving parties with a combined world-wide turnover of more than 5 billion ecu (around £3.5 billion) are subject to the control of the European Commission, provided that the EC turnover of each of at least two companies involved exceeds 250 million ecu (around £175 million) and the companies concerned do not have at least two-thirds of their EC turnover from the same member state.[1]

Mergers which are not caught by the EC Merger Regulation remain subject to national competition law. There are however some circumstances in which jurisdiction even over mergers with an EC dimension may revert to the national competition authorities. A member state can intervene under Article 21 of the Regulation on grounds of public security, prudential controls or diversity of the media to prevent a merger which the European Commission would otherwise have cleared. It may also request the European Commission under Article 9 to refer a merger back for assessment by the national competition authorities. For such an application to succeed the member state must demonstrate to the European Commission that the concentration threatens to create or to strengthen a dominant position significantly impeding competition in a distinct market in its territory. In such a case the European Commission decides, after preliminary inquiries, whether to deal with the matter itself or to refer some or all issues arising under it to these national authorities. So far there has only been one successful application for national jurisdiction under these provisions: the proposed joint venture between Steetley plc and Tarmac plc which the European Commission referred back to the United Kingdom in March 1992 in respect of certain specific regional and national product markets.

---

[1] See the DTI's booklet, *Merger Control in Europe: the main provisions of EC regulation 4064/89*.

FURTHER READING

Monopolies and Mergers Commission. 1991 Review. Available free from the Commission.

Assessing Competition. Available free from the Commission.

Fact Sheets. A series of six fact sheets describing the Commission and its work is also available free from the Commission.

Annual Report of the Director General of Fair Trading 1991. HMSO. 1992. ISBN 0 10 203893 7   £12.00.

Mergers Policy: a Department of Trade and Industry Paper on the policy and procedures of merger control. HMSO. 1988. ISBN 0 11 513999 0   £4.30.

Opening Markets: New Policy on Restrictive Trade Practices. HMSO. 1989. Cm 727 ISBN 0 10 107272 4   £6.20.

Mergers: A guide to the procedures under the Fair Trading Act 1973. 1991. A free booklet issued by the Office of Fair Trading.

Anti-competitive practices: a guide to the provisions of the Competition Act 1980. 1986. A booklet issued by the Office of Fair Trading.

The Monopolies and Mergers Yearbook edited by Robert Miller. Blackwell. 1991. ISBN 0 631 18194 6   £125.

Gardner, N. *A Guide to United Kingdom and European Community Competition Policy.* Macmillan. 1990. ISBN 0 33 349048 7   £40.00.

Goyder, D. G. *EEC Competition Law.* Oxford: Clarendon Press. 1988. ISBN 0 19 825403 2   £20.00.

Vickers, J and Yarrow, G. *Privatisation: an economic analysis.* The MIT Press. 1988. ISBN 0 262 72011 6   £14.95.

Whish, R. *Competition Law.* London: Butterworths. 1989. 2nd ed. ISBN 0 40 601280 6   £25.00.

The legal framework under which the Commission principally operates is set out in two Acts of Parliament:

The Fair Trading Act 1973. HMSO. ISBN 0 10 544173 2   £8.00.

The Competition Act 1980. HMSO. ISBN 0 10 542180 4   £2.25.

A list of Commission reports is available on request from the Monopolies and Mergers Commission. Current MMC reports can be purchased from:

HMSO Bookshop
49 High Holborn
London
WC1V 6HB

and by mail and telephone order from:

HMSO Publications Centre
PO Box 276
London
SW8 5DT.

Contact points:

Press office: 071-324 1407
Library: 071-324 1467

Printed in the United Kingdom for HMSO
Dd 294913 C120 7/92